The Journey

A Richard Jackson Book

Japanese Americans,
Racism, and Renewal

The Journey

Painting and text by
Sheila Hamanaka

Book design by
Steve Frederick

Orchard Books   New York

Orchard Books
A division of Franklin Watts, Inc.
387 Park Avenue South
New York, NY 10016

Manufactured in the United States of America.
Printed by General Offset Co., Inc.
Bound by Horowitz / Rae.
Book design by Steve Frederick

10 9 8 7 6 5 4 3 2 1

The text of this book is set in 14 pt. Rotation.
The illustration is a five-panel
oil painting, reproduced
in full color.
Library of Congress Cataloging-in-Publication Data
Hamanaka, Sheila.
The journey / Sheila Hamanaka.
p.   cm.
Summary: Text and photographed details of a mural depict the
history of the Japanese people in America.
ISBN 0-531-05849-2.—ISBN 0-531-08449-3 (lib. bdg.)
1. Japanese Americans—History—Juvenile literature.   2. Japanese
Americans—History—Pictorial works—Juvenile literature.
[1. Japanese American—History.]   I. Title.
E184.J3H35   1990
973'.04956—dc20
89-22877 CIP AC

For my mother,
Mary Fumiko Sasaki Hamanaka

Acknowledgments:

Kiyoshi Hamanaka Davis
Suzuko Hamanaka Davis
Conrad Kiyoshi Hamanaka
Lionelle Hamanaka
Aiko Yoshinaga Herzig
Jonathan and Lillian Hill
Keiko Hirano
William Hohri
Dick Jackson
Teru Kanazawa
Tooru Kanazawa
Lauren Miller
Phil Nash
Akira Tana
Emi Tonooka
Ron Yamamoto
The Japanese American Citizens' League
and the staff at Orchard Books

Japanese immigrants first sailed across the Pacific to Hawaii and America in the late 1800s. They were lured by the possibility of owning land and the promise of farm or factory work; but, like the Chinese before them, they met with prejudice. American farmers of European descent and the unions fought for alien land laws (passed in California in 1913 and not repealed until 1952) which made it illegal for first-generation Japanese Americans to own a home, a farm, or a grocery store. They were prevented from becoming citizens or marrying Americans of European ancestry. In 1924, the U.S. Congress slammed shut "the golden door," and all immigration from Japan was halted.

The Journey, a five-panel mural measuring eight feet by twenty-five feet, is a painting about Japanese American history, and a personal inquiry focusing on events that changed my family's life.

During World War II, from 1941 to 1945, the Issei (*ee-say*), the first generation of Japanese to arrive in America, and the Nisei (*nee-say*), their American-born children, endured an outrage largely kept hidden from the public—and from my generation, the Sansei (*sahn-say*). I was born after the war, in 1949, and grew up unaware that my grandfather had died in a concentration camp, not in Europe or Japan, but in America. His crime—and the crime of 120,000 others: being of Japanese ancestry.

In the folklore of Japan there is a story about Momotaro, the Peach Boy. A childless couple find a peach. They open the fruit and out jumps a little boy who chases away demons. I painted *The Journey* to open the past, hoping to help chase away the demons of prejudice and injustice.

S.H.

5

*A*merica: land of plenty. Peaches. Pears. Strawberries. Lettuce....Plenty of work for the Japanese, who were excluded from union jobs. Plenty of work— but little pay. In the late 1930s my father toiled in the fields ten hours a day, six days a week, for twenty-five cents an hour. Many Issei had struggled to help their Nisei children through college, but racial discrimination forced most of the graduates back to the fields or to employment as domestic servants or gardeners. The few Japanese able to purchase farms were restricted, because of prejudice, to the poorest land, near deserts, swamps, railroads, or airports. But they brought from their home islands years of agricultural experience. By 1941, the land they had enriched was worth $280 an acre, compared to $38 for other farmland on the West Coast.

Above: Excluded from trades and professions, Japanese worked as "stoop laborers" picking crops: as early as 1915, they were providing 75 percent of the fresh produce consumed in Los Angeles.

Opposite: Japanese fisherpeople became major suppliers of tuna and along with Japanese abalone divers helped build the West Coast seafood industry. Other workers had to take what factory jobs they could find, such as canning fish or pineapple.

At night, the Japanese went home to segregation. American city residents of European ancestry fought against integrated neighborhoods. "Little Tokyos" sprang up in Los Angeles, San Francisco, Sacramento, and Seattle—wherever there were sizable Japanese populations. The new immigrants sought safety and camaraderie by flocking to restaurants like the one my grandfather owned, as well as to theaters, Buddhist temples and Christian churches, sumo wrestling tournaments and baseball games. Outside these communities, newspapers sided with farmers, businesses, and unions in hostilely labeling Japanese Americans "The Yellow Peril."

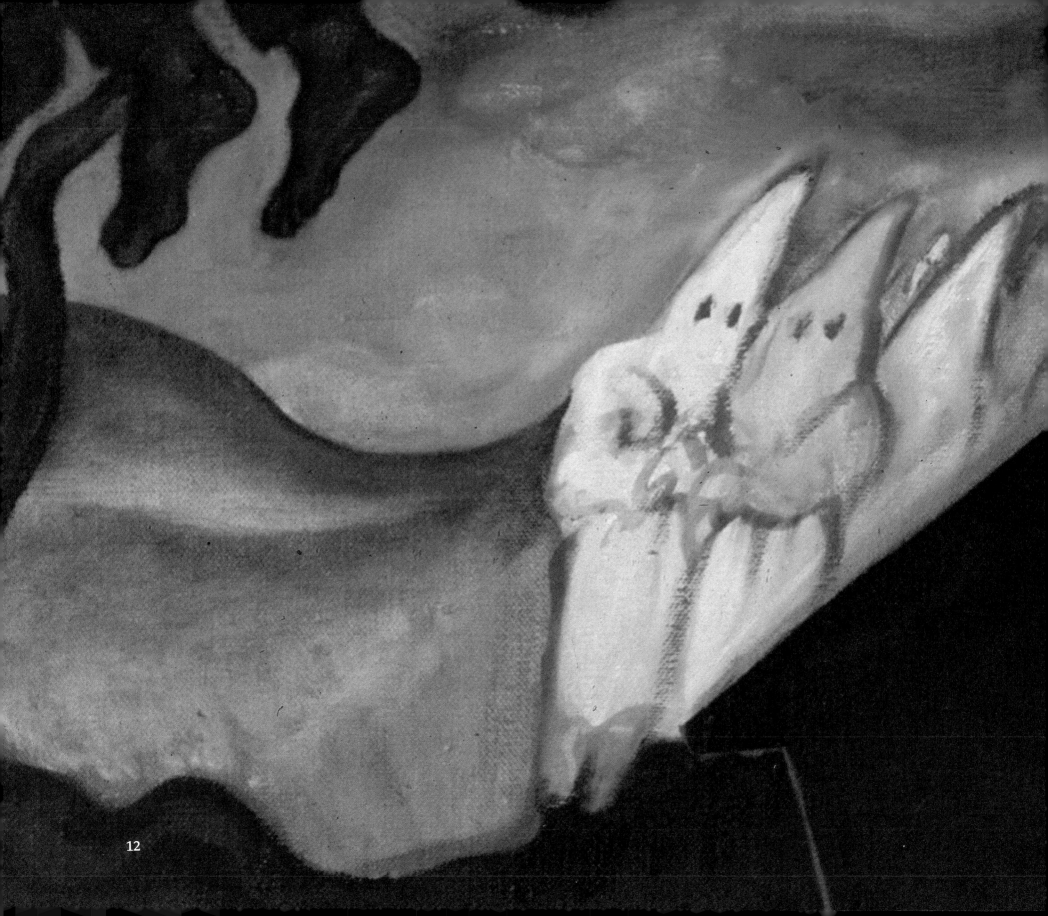

America in 1941 was a land of lynchings. The Ku Klux Klan rode freely in the South. Schools, buses, restaurants, theaters, drinking fountains, blood banks, as well as neighborhoods and the U.S. Armed Forces, were racially segregated.

December 7, 1941: The Japanese Imperial Navy bombed the U.S. Pacific Fleet at Pearl Harbor, a naval base in Hawaii. Within hours, FBI agents were knocking on doors, arresting many prominent members of Japanese American communities along the West Coast: ministers, businesspeople, newspaper editors, farmers, fisherpeople, instructors of judo and flower arrangement. They and their families were not told where they were being taken or when they would be back. On December 8, the United States declared war on Japan.

December 11, 1941: U.S. Secretary of War Henry L. Stimson proclaimed eight western states to be a "theater of operations" under military control, commanded by Lieutenant General John L. DeWitt. The same day, the U.S. declared war on Germany and Italy.

February 19, 1942: President Franklin D. Roosevelt, himself a believer in the racial inferiority of the Japanese, issued Executive Order 9066. All persons of Japanese ancestry living on the West Coast, including seventy thousand American-born citizens, were condemned to concentration camps without trial or hearing. Skirting the Constitution, Colonel Karl R. Bendetsen had devised a plan stating that it was a "military necessity" to remove the Japanese from an area now under military control.

Painted as Japanese Bunraku puppets, U.S. politicians and military personnel play in the "theater of war." Behind them lurk the Kuro-maku—the word means "puppet masters" but also "political manipulators." Right, top: Provost Marshal Allen W. Gullion, General DeWitt, Colonel Bendetsen. Right, below: President Roosevelt, Secretary of War Stimson, and Assistant Secretary of War John J. McCloy.

"A Jap is a Jap," declared General DeWitt in the racial slur publicly accepted at the time. Earl Warren, the Attorney General of California and later Chief Justice of the Supreme Court, insisted that the fact no Japanese Americans had committed any act of sabotage was sure proof that they would do so in the future. Some pointed to Japanese American farms next to railroads and airports as proof of conspiracy. Though no detention was ordered during the war for German or Italian Americans as ethnic groups, anyone as little as one-sixteenth Japanese was to be imprisoned, even infant orphans—except in Hawaii, where the 158,000 members of the "enemy race" were needed to staff the military bases and run the economy. On the West Coast, Japanese American families were given only two days to two weeks to dispose of their homes, farms, businesses, belongings, and pets.

"April 1, 1942: INSTRUCTIONS TO ALL PERSONS OF JAPANESE ANCESTRY: All Japanese persons both alien and non-alien will be evacuated from the above designated area by 12:00 o'clock noon on Tuesday, April 7, 1942."

Land that the Japanese had nurtured for years was gobbled up by greedy farmers. Desperate, people sold possessions for next to nothing. A thirty-seven-room hotel went for three hundred dollars. Whatever couldn't be sold or placed in the care of friends had to be abandoned. In the panic, precious books, mementos, and Japanese antiques were burned. A columnist for the *San Francisco Examiner* wrote: "Herd 'em up, pack 'em off, and give 'em the inside room in the badlands. Let 'em be hurt, hungry, and dead up against it….Personally, I hate the Japanese. And that goes for all of them." Tagged and numbered, families were first shipped to assembly centers such as the Santa Anita racetrack and forced to live in horse stalls. From there they were loaded onto trains, and, with shades drawn, taken under armed guard to "the badlands."

*Silhouette of a concentration camp barrack.
There were ten camps: Manzanar, California;
Tule Lake, California; Poston, Arizona; Gila,
Arizona; Minidoka, Idaho; Heart Mountain,
Wyoming; Granada, Colorado; Topaz, Utah;
Rohwer, Arkansas; and Jerome, Arkansas.*

Concentration camps were hastily erected on Indian reservations or swamp and desert wasteland. Blistered by heat in the day, numbed with cold at night, one family and sometimes two lived in a single room in row after row of four- to six-room tar-paper shacks without running water. Public latrines that lacked any privacy, inadequate medical care, and food served in mass mess halls eroded morale and family life. Those who worked full-time were paid twelve to nineteen dollars a month. Anyone, including the elderly and children, who wandered too close to the barbed-wire fences surrounding the camps risked being shot by guards who sat in towers, armed with rifles and machine guns.

In 1942, one woman and three men raised constitutional challenges to their imprisonment in separate cases that finally reached the Supreme Court.

Above (left to right): Mitsuye Endo, Gordon Kiyoshi Hirabayashi, lawyer Wayne Collins, Minoru Yasui, and Fred Toyasaburo Korematsu. They wear the masks of traditional Japanese Noh drama and are in the pose symbolizing Enlightenment.

Right: Anti-Japanese politicians and journalists (top to bottom): Attorney General of California Earl Warren, newspaper publisher William Randolph Hearst, Representative Martin Dies, newspaper columnist Walter Lippmann. In the far right Nazi defendants at the Nuremberg War Crimes trial use U.S. Supreme Court decisions against Hirabayashi and Korematsu to justify their own concentration camps for the Jews.

Lloyd L. Cosgrove, head of the European American supremacist group Native Sons of the Golden West.

My older sister was two and my brother
six when they were imprisoned at the
camp in Jerome, Arkansas.

November 19, 1942: Japanese American prisoners commenced a general strike at the camp in Poston, Arizona.

December 5, 1942: U.S. Military Police opened fire on Japanese American protestors at the Manzanar Relocation Center in California. Two dead. Eight wounded.

As the war in Europe intensified, the U.S. Government began to conscript the Japanese it had earlier labeled "enemy aliens." In 1943, all prisoners in the camps over the age of seventeen were ordered to fill out Loyalty Questionnaires. Would you serve in combat wherever sent? they were asked. Old people and women worried they would be drafted. Also asked: Will you foreswear allegiance to the Japanese emperor, Hirohito? Prohibited by law from becoming U.S. citizens, Issei feared they would be people without a country. The majority answered "yes," but some answered "no" as a form of protest, or to avoid being separated from their parents: those who did were labeled "disloyal" and shipped to Tule Lake, where they were guarded by a full battalion of 920 and six tanks. Strikes followed the camp administration's denial of a public funeral for a prisoner killed in an accident. Riots erupted over camp employees stealing truckloads of food. When Dillon Myer, the National Director of the camps, visited Tule Lake, he was met by five thousand prisoners protesting camp conditions. In all the camps, bitter fighting broke out between those anxious to prove their loyalty to the United States and others angered over their imprisonment. Several hundred men refused to support a country that had violated their basic rights: 263 Japanese Americans were sentenced to prison for resisting the draft.

May 1944: In Tule Lake, Shoichi James Okamoto was unjustifiably killed by a sentry who was then fined one dollar for the unauthorized expenditure of U.S. property—the bullet.

25

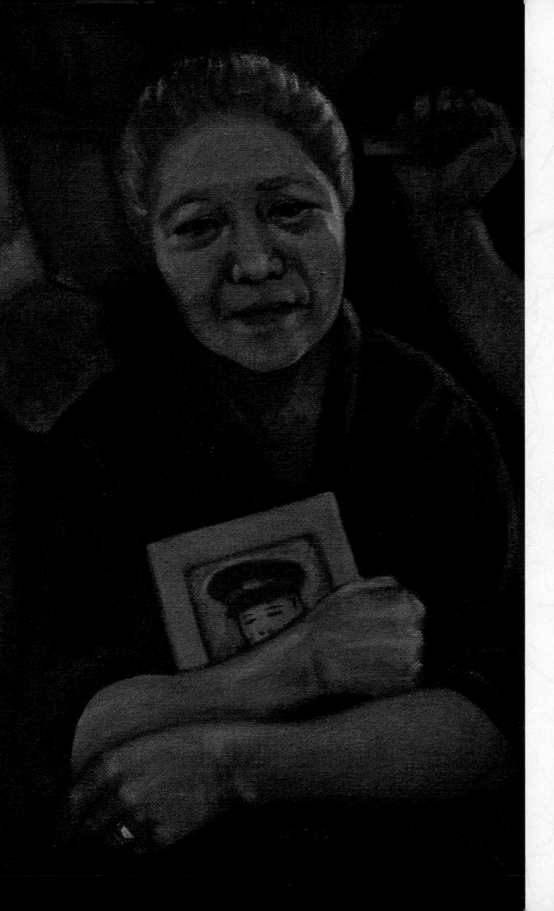

In October 1944, the all-Nisei unit composed of the Hawaiian 100th Infantry and the 442nd Regimental Combat Team suffered more than eight hundred casualties rescuing from Nazi forces in France some two hundred Texans of the "Lost Battalion." The unit lived up to its slogan, "Go for broke," suffering a casualty rate five times greater than the average for other regimental combat teams and becoming the most highly decorated in U.S. military history. The thirty-three thousand Japanese Americans who fought for the United States proved their loyalty. Thousands served in the Pacific in the war against their ancestral islands, most working for military intelligence or serving as interpreters. At home, where they were outcasts in their own country, the families of fallen Japanese American soldiers had a double grief to bear: the death of loved ones, and homelessness.

April 29, 1945: Their families imprisoned at home, Japanese American soldiers helped liberate Dachau, the Nazi concentration camp.

Overleaf: Hiroshima, August 6, 1945: America drops the first atomic bomb: it burns like a small sun over the city, the heat at the center of the blast reaching three hundred thousand degrees.

August 9, 1945: A second atomic bomb is dropped, on Nagasaki.

September 2, 1945: Japan surrendered. World War II was over. More than 630,000 people had been exposed to the heat and radiation of the two atomic bombs. The most fortunate victims died immediately. Black raindrops, swollen with radioactive ash, fell on survivors, whose burned skin peeled off and hung in shreds. After a year, the death toll climbed to two hundred thousand.

Meanwhile, seven out of ten Nisei at Tule Lake renounced their U.S. citizenship. A lifetime of discrimination and finally imprisonment caused twenty thousand people to apply for repatriation to Japan. Eight thousand actually went. But like the banished Noh character Yoroboshi, many regretted decisions made under painful pressure and sought to return to America. Some families were separated for as long as fifteen years.

March 20, 1946: The last Japanese Americans left the concentration camps, each given twenty-five dollars and a ride home; but many of their homes had been burned to the ground by racists. Scores of camp survivors had contracted tuberculosis. Others suffered the effects of nervous breakdowns, or later died from aggravated heart conditions. Burdened by shame and grief, most walled off the past with silence. But a few protested publicly. In 1948, the Evacuation Claims Act was passed. Those who could show proof of loss were paid ten cents on every dollar, at 1942 value, averaging about $340 per victim.

In 1952 the Japanese American Citizens' League lobbied for and helped gain passage of the McCarran-Walter Act, which enabled Japanese immigrants to apply for citizenship.

But even as the first Issei swore their loyalty, concentration camps were again being built in secret—one at Tule Lake—under Title II of the Internal Security Act of 1950, called the Emergency Detention Act. Conservatives led by Senator Joseph R. McCarthy were at the time conducting hearings in Washington, D.C., to intimidate anyone who might disagree with the government. The new camps were planned for such "Communists." In 1971, the Emergency Detention Act was repealed in a bill fought for by Senator Daniel Inouye and Representative (later Senator) Spark Matsunaga, both 100th/442nd veterans.

Political unrest in America in the 1960s and 70s inspired the Japanese American struggle to win an apology and monetary reparations from the U.S. Government. At last, Momotaro was ready to spring from the peach....

Early 1950s: 100th/442nd veterans and others demand citizenship rights for their parents.

1960s: The African American Civil Rights Movement.

Late 1960s / early 1970s: The Anti-Vietnam War Movement.

parked by the Japanese American Citizens' League's Seattle chapter, scores of citizens' committees sprouted around the country, among them the JACL's National Committee for Redress, the National Council for Japanese American Redress, and the National Coalition for Redress and Reparations. A mass campaign grew with support from Democrats and Republicans, veterans' groups, social activists, and churches. In 1983, Hirabayashi, Yasui, and Korematsu reopened the cases which they had lost before the Supreme Court in 1943 and 1944. Their lawyers gained access to secret files and proved that officials from the Departments of War and Justice had lied to the court and destroyed evidence in order to justify the camps as a "military necessity." The facts supporting the earlier convictions of the three men were seen to be deliberate falsehoods: the men were finally cleared by judges in Washington, California, and Oregon. During the war, the Supreme Court had ruled in Endo's case that the detention of a concededly loyal citizen was unconstitutional. But in all cases the court failed to strike down the legality of the military order which forced the Japanese into camps. Justice Robert Jackson had voiced a dissenting view in 1944: "Once a judicial opinion…rationalizes the Constitution to show that the Constitution sanctions such an order, the Court for all time has validated the principle of racial discrimination in criminal procedure and of transplanting American citizens. The principle then lies about like a loaded weapon."

In 1988, after public hearings run by the Commission of Wartime Relocation and Internment of Civilians, the government formally apologized to Japanese Americans: surviving victims of the camps were to be paid twenty thousand dollars each.

Opposite: Demonstrators display banners protesting the eviction of elderly Japanese Americans from hotels in Los Angeles's Little Tokyo in 1977.

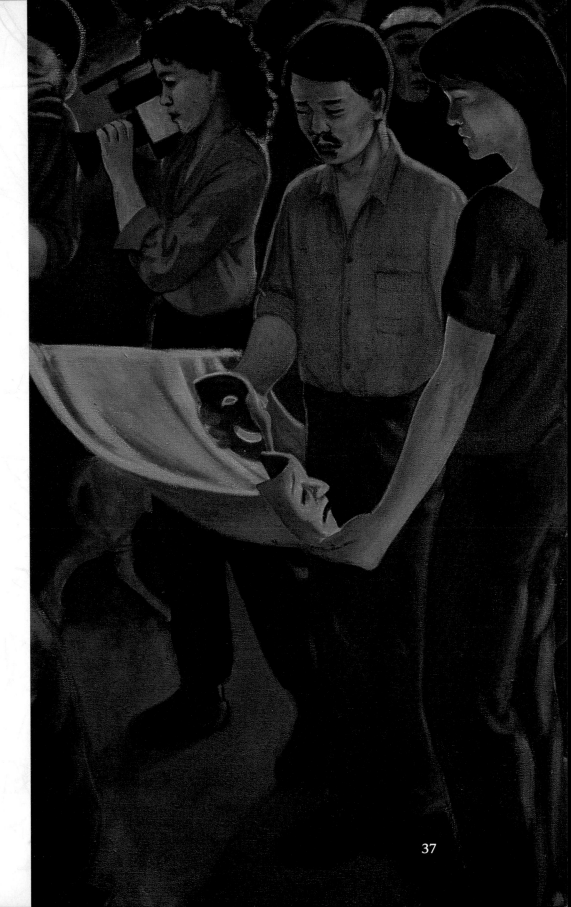

he Journey begins with an Issei mother looking fearfully toward events to come. It pauses as the Sansei remove their own masks and look back, some assuming the Noh gestures of Grief and Enlightenment. The past is seen unfolding in a theater because so often what we take to be the truth of history and the honesty of law is made up, a performance. Demonstrators surging forward are being led by the fourth generation, the Yonsei (*yon-say*). As I write, the Japanese American community still works to see that reparations are actually paid: Half of the camp survivors have already died. In the painting's final panel, one man's shirt bears swallows, a symbol of the repayment of debt; a boy's T-shirt, a wave—symbol of power and resilience. And floating before us, a carp, the symbol of renewal.